AF324212

Books on Books 5-
459269

THE
COPP CLARK CO
LIMITED
517

OZ IN CANADA

A Bibliography

C.J. Hinke

Introduction by Peter E. Hanff

William Hoffer

VANCOUVER

OZ IN CANADA

COPYRIGHT © 1982 C.J. HINKE

ISBN: 0-919758-00-2

1. BAUM, L. FRANK (LYMAN FRANK), 1856-1919—BIBLIOGRAPHY. 2. THOMPSON, RUTH PLUMLY, 1893-1976—BIBLIOGRAPHY. 3. CANADA—IMPRINTS. 4. ENGLISH IMPRINTS—CANADA. 5. COPP CLARK COMPANY. I. TITLE.

Z8080.H56	016.813'4	C82-091106-2
LOC. CLASS NO.	DEWEY DEC. NO.	CANADIANA CONTROL NO.

PUBLISHED BY WILLIAM HOFFER
570 GRANVILLE STREET
VANCOUVER CANADA

PRODUCTION: BASELINE PUBLICATION TRADES COOPERATIVE
COVER: DOUG BROWN
PHOTOGRAPHY: GLEN ERIKSON

PRINTED AND BOUND IN CANADA

TABLE OF CONTENTS

(*Table of Contents* continued)

FOR
SARAH & SIMON

INTRODUCTION

Well, My Dears: Here I am again to say, How do you do and how do you do it? How do *you manage to write such jolly letters about Oz? From every state and Canada they have come pouring in to make me happy and, as Ozma remarked to the Scarecrow, when I showed them all to her, "Why we have as many loyal subjects outside of Oz as we have here in the country."*—from Ruth Plumly Thompson's July 1926 introduction to *The Hungry Tiger of Oz*

Experienced collectors of early editions of the Oz books have long recognized that many titles were apparently issued in Canada in forms nearly identical to the original American editions. Indeed, most large collections of Oz books have a least a copy or two of the Canadian issues, but their general scarcity made it difficult to understand just how many such Canadian issues occurred and which titles were actually published in Canada.

The authors of *Bibliographia Oziana: A Concise Bibliographical Checklist of the Oz Books by L. Frank Baum and His Successors* did not have the opportunity of examining very many copies of Canadian issues and chose to describe them in only cursory fashion. Therefore these bibliographers welcomed C.J.Hinke's pioneering effort and diligence in tracking down Canadian issues and describing them in detail for the first time. Although historical records between the cooperating publishers, Reilly & Britton (later Reilly & Lee) of Chicago and The Copp Clark Company of Toronto were sadly lacking, Mr. Hinke has brought together a surprising amount of information regarding the original publication of the Oz books in Canada. His work is a valuable contribution both to the history of publishing in Canada and to the bibliography of the Oz books.

Perhaps the most exciting bibliographical discovery made during the course of Mr. Hinke's research were Canadian copies of the first edition of *Ozma of Oz* published in 1907. A review of that title was preserved in L. Frank Baum's scrapbook and appeared to indicate that Copp, Clark had issued a version of the book, but no copy had ever been seen and it appeared possible that the Canadian firm had merely distributed Reilly & Britton copies in Canada. Mr. Hinke offers here, the first full description of the Canadian issue of *Ozma of Oz*, evidently the earliest of the Oz series published as a joint venture of the Chicago and Toronto publishers.

—Peter E. Hanff
President,
The International Wizard of Oz Club
February 1982

THE COPP, CLARK STORY

THE COPP, CLARK STORY

In 1879, William Copp and Henry Clark bought out a Toronto publishing house that traced its history back to 1841. They renamed the company Copp, Clark & Company Limited. Changing typographical fashions over the years resulted in occasional modifications of the firm's imprint. From about 1900, the company was usually designated The Copp, Clark Company, Limited, and by the 1940's, the usual imprint was The Copp Clark Company or more simply, Copp Clark. Since 1963, Copp Clark has been owned by the English holding company, Sir Isaac Pitman & Sons, Ltd., and the present head of the Toronto firm is Michael I. Pitman. In this article, the company is referred to simply as Copp Clark except when specifically referring to one of its earlier imprint styles.

For many years The Copp Clark Company, Limited, Publishers, of Toronto, published the Oz series under their imprint. The Reilly & Britton Company (later Reilly & Lee) of Chicago provided the copies for Canadian issue and produced them with specially printed bindings and title pages. With one possible exception, the Copp Clark copies were produced from the original printing of each title.

A newspaper clipping in L. Frank Baum's own scrapbook refers to copies of *Ozma of Oz* as published by Copp Clark in 1907, the

Canadian firm distributing copies produced by Reilly & Britton. This earliest recorded Canadian issue of an Oz book bears no spine imprint, has a Canadian cancel title page and blank copyright page verso.

The Chicago publishers supplied Copp Clark with copies of each new Oz book upon publication from 1907 to 1931, with the possible exception of *The Road to Oz* in 1909 for which no early Canadian copy has been discovered. The Canadian issues ended with Ruth Plumly Thompson's *Pirates in Oz*. In 1931, the Canadian Copyright Act was amended to permit copyright protection of all original works, irrespective of country of origin. Prior to 1931, only books "first published within His Majesty's Dominions" were protected.

Reilly & Britton/Reilly & Lee distributed other titles from its lists through the auspices of Copp Clark. Although there has been no attempt to include them here, several Canadian issues of titles illustrated by John R. Neill have been discovered and more may well come to light.

The original Oz books issued by Copp Clark were made up by the Chicago publisher from sheets of the first printing and were evidently issued in Canada simultaneously with their first U.S. publication. The singular exception, *The Patchwork Girl of Oz* (1913), the Canadian issue of which has what is believed to be the later positioning of the heading "Chap. Three," may provide bibliographical evidence that the two variant forms in U.S. and Canadian editions resulted from a stop-press correction made during the first press run.

The copies prepared for Canadian issue generally were modified by substituting a binding bearing a Copp Clark imprint on the spine and by substituting the Copp Clark imprint on the title page for that of Reilly & Britton/Reilly & Lee. Whether this was accomplished by substituting an entire specially-printed title gathering or by a stop-press change of the printing plate for the title page has not been determined. Although the remainder of each book is identical to its first U.S. issue, the existence of a modified copyright page in *Rinkitink in Oz* (1916) tends to support the former possibility.

Copp Clark copies are very scarce and too few have been available for examination to allow generalisation safely beyond the basic outline given above. Nevertheless, specific variations in the general pattern include *Rinkitink in Oz* (1916), Canadian copies of which have a line, "Made in U.S.A.", added to the copyright page, and *The Gnome King of Oz* (1927), copies of which have either of two different Copp Clark imprints on the integral title page, perhaps resulting from damage to the original printing plate: no priority has been determined.

No records indicating the actual number of copies prepared for Canadian issue have yet been discovered. We know only that no later states have been discovered except as printer's or binder's errors. The descriptions presented here have in many cases been based on a single surviving Copp Clark copy; in all other instances no more than a few copies have been available for examination. Collectors of Oz books have long recognised that Copp Clark copies are very scarce.

Copp Clark issued another Baum title, *Queen Zixi of Ix* in 1905 for The Century Company of New York, publishers of *St. Nicholas Magazine,* in which the book first appeared in serial form. Still another work, Baum's anonymous novel for adults, *The Last Egyptian* (1908), was issued by William Briggs of Toronto for the Philadelphia publisher, Edward Stern & Co.

In 1960, two new Copp Clark variants were inadvertently created when the original Canadian printing plates were used to print the title pages of new impressions of *Glinda of Oz* and *The Cowardly Lion of Oz*. Reilly & Lee was at that time reprinting the entire Oz series. The new volumes were rather thin without the traditional colour-printed paste-down labels on the front covers; their spines were stamped with the usual information and with the fancy, semi-script spine imprint (cf. page 20, *Bibliographia Oziana*). The volumes were issued in dustjackets by a variety of designers, including several by Dick Martin. It was thought for many years that only six copies of each of these two titles escaped being withdrawn, but collectors have discovered more. One incident connected with this printing of the Oz books is worth recounting because it reveals something of the exigencies of book publishing and shows how a variant may be created. Although the paste-down cover labels had been deliberately omitted from this printing of the Oz books, Reilly & Lee decided to display a group of the books at the American Booksellers Association convention. In error, a group of Oz books received labels hurriedly hand-cut from the dust jackets and pasted to the front covers of the books. At least one of these was a copy of *Glinda of Oz* with the Copp Clark imprint.

About 1941, Copp Clark began to produce the early Oz titles in Canada. These were apparently made up from photographic reproductions of the original U.S. copies. Only *The Land of Oz, Ozma of Oz, Dorothy and the Wizard in Oz* and *The Road to Oz* were manufactured in Canada, and they were printed on decidedly cheap wartime paper. They were offered at a lower price than the "regular editions" of the rest of the series imported from the U.S. There seem to be many surviving examples of these Canadian-manufactured copies, despite the very noticeable yellowing of the pages.

THE CANADIAN EDITIONS OF THE OZ BOOKS

A CHECKLIST OF THE CANADIAN EDITIONS OF THE OZ BOOKS

The scarcity of copies of the Canadian editions of Oz books precluded more than occasional and incomplete listing without description or comment in *Bibliographia Oziana*. This excellent bibliography by Peter E. Hanff, Douglas G. Greene, Dick Martin, James E. Haff and David L. Greene was first published in 1976 by The International Wizard of Oz Club, Inc., P.O. Box 95, Kinderhook, Ill. 62345 USA. For purposes of brevity, the first Canadian editions are described as being "identical to first U.S. state"; for exhaustive and complete descriptions of first U.S. editions, readers will be directed to consult *Bibliographia Oziana*. Though long out of print, the bibliography was reprinted by the Oz Club in 1981. In keeping with the plan of that volume, only characteristics unique and peculiar to the Canadian issues are normally given, except as noted in the text.

In order to keep the checklist itself as brief as possible, the various imprints used by Copp Clark have been classified and are reproduced here. Readers should bear in mind that because the various imprints were typeset specifically for each title, and that the printing surface or binding and the depth of impression vary with each title, the categories given here are only representative of the various styles used.

Every attempt has been made to reproduce the imprints in identical size and manner to those used on the books themselves.

The listing is presented in canonical order so that it will most readily conform to the sequence of books given in Bibliographia Oziana. Reference numbers follow each title.

The International Wizard of Oz Club was founded in 1957 to bring together all those interested in L. Frank Baum and Oz, and today has nearly 2000 members.

Membership includes a subscription to THE BAUM BUGLE: A JOURNAL OF OZ, published quarterly. Each issue contains items of biography, bibliography, rare reproductions and comment.

Membership is currently (1982) $10 U.S. annually.

The International Wizard of Oz Club
Post Office Box 95
Kinderhook, Illinois 62345
USA

THE LAND OF OZ

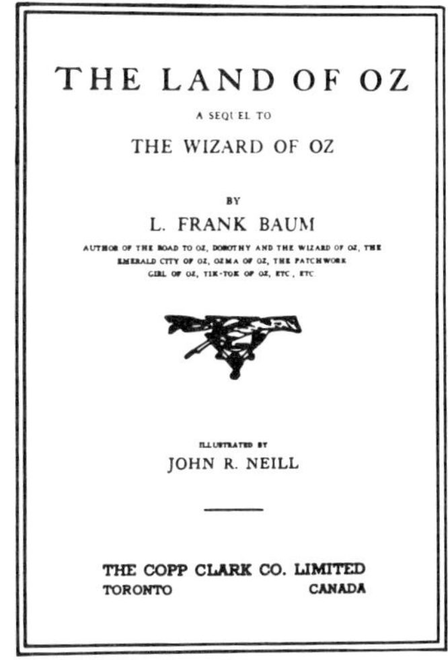
THE LAND OF OZ

A SEQUEL TO

THE WIZARD OF OZ

BY

L. FRANK BAUM

AUTHOR OF THE ROAD TO OZ, DOROTHY AND THE WIZARD OF OZ, THE EMERALD CITY OF OZ, OZMA OF OZ, THE PATCHWORK GIRL OF OZ, TIK-TOK OF OZ, ETC., ETC

ILLUSTRATED BY

JOHN R. NEILL

THE COPP CLARK CO. LIMITED
TORONTO CANADA

The first recorded Canadian publication of *The Land of Oz* was also the first printed in Canada. About 1941, The Copp Clark Co., Ltd., of Toronto, published *The Land of Oz, Ozma of Oz, Dorothy and the Wizard in Oz* and *The Road to Oz,* all printed on cheap, wartime paper. Numerous copies survive, despite the noticeable yellowing of the paper. The books were similar to the then-current popular editions printed in the United States, though slightly reduced in size and format. All had colour pictorial paper paste-down labels on the front covers. The spine imprints read: COPP / CLARK. All four titles had blank endpapers. Three titles, *The Land of Oz, Ozma of Oz* and *The Road to Oz* have title-page imprints reading: THE COPP CLARK CO. LIMITED / TORONTO CANADA. Other unique characteristics of this series are described under the appropriate listing below. The dust jackets of three of the four titles, *The Land of Oz, Dorothy and the Wizard in Oz* and *The Road to Oz,* list these titles with asterisks on both front and back flaps, explained at the bottom of the flaps as "*Made in Canada." Evidently these were the first actual Canadian printings of the Oz books. The remaining titles in the Oz series, presumably imported, are listed as "REGULAR EDITIONS". (Bib Oz. II; Schiller 109)

OZMA OF OZ

1907, identical to first American state, but having no publisher's spine imprint. The endpapers are blank. The cancel title page bears imprint 1, as below, and the verso is blank. The book has no copyright notation. The fifth line of the "Author's Notes" has the "O" present in "Ozma"; the illustration on page (221) is in colour and pages 135-(136), 153-154, and (221)-222 are integral. A review appeared in the Toronto *Christian Guardian,* December 13,

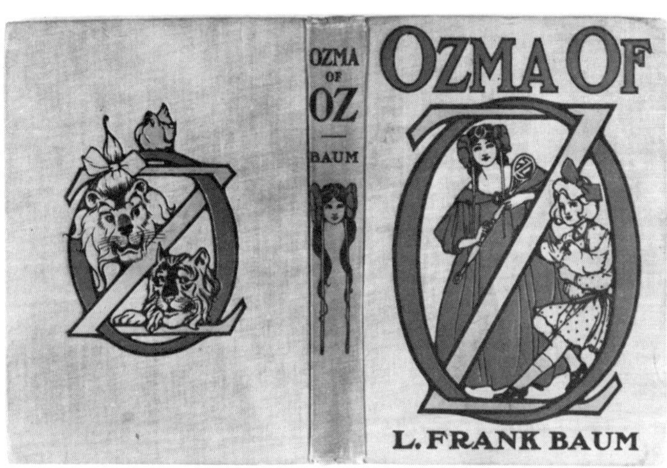

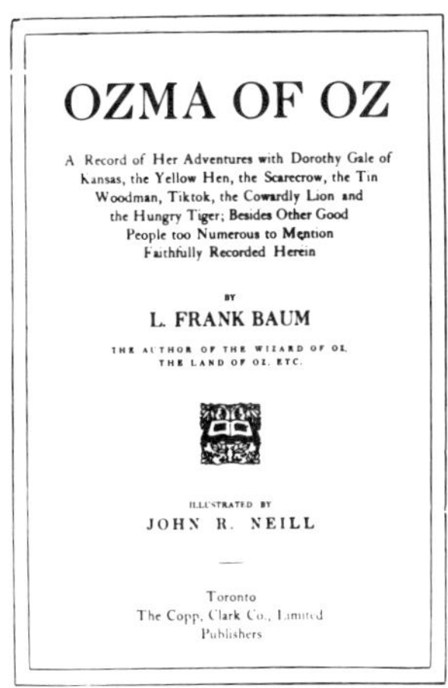

OZMA OF OZ

A Record of Her Adventures with Dorothy Gale of Kansas, the Yellow Hen, the Scarecrow, the Tin Woodman, Tiktok, the Cowardly Lion and the Hungry Tiger; Besides Other Good People too Numerous to Mention Faithfully Recorded Herein

BY

L. FRANK BAUM

THE AUTHOR OF THE WIZARD OF OZ, THE LAND OF OZ, ETC.

ILLUSTRATED BY

JOHN R. NEILL

Toronto
The Copp, Clark Co., Limited
Publishers

1907, which survives in L. Frank Baum's scrapbook of reviews of his books. Title-page imprint 1.

Spine imprint: Blank

Title page: Toronto/The Copp, Clark Co., Limited/Publishers

Later printing

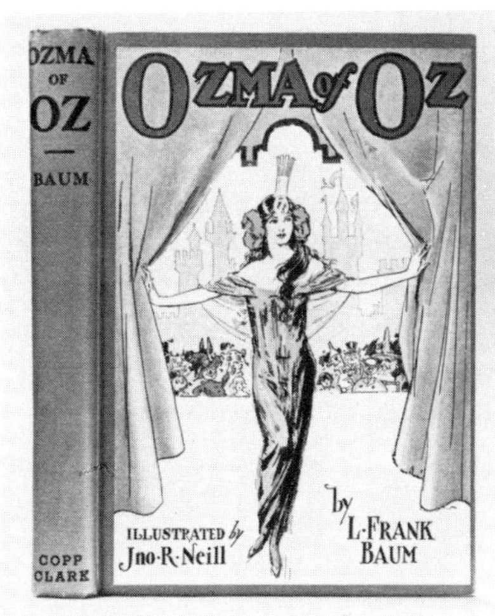

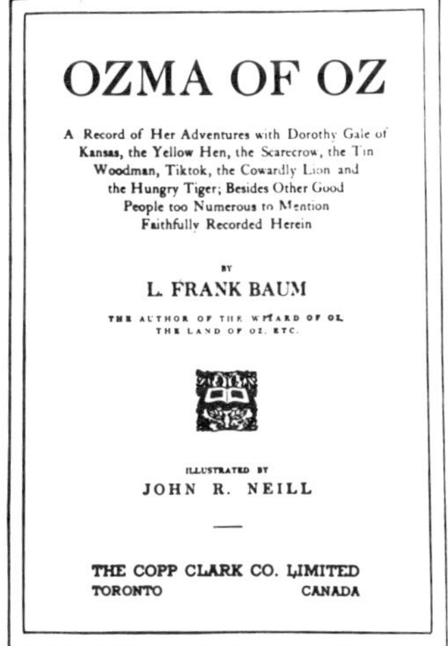

OZMA OF OZ

A Record of Her Adventures with Dorothy Gale of Kansas, the Yellow Hen, the Scarecrow, the Tin Woodman, Tiktok, the Cowardly Lion and the Hungry Tiger; Besides Other Good People too Numerous to Mention Faithfully Recorded Herein

BY

L. FRANK BAUM

THE AUTHOR OF THE WIZARD OF OZ, THE LAND OF OZ, ETC.

ILLUSTRATED BY

JOHN R. NEILL

THE COPP CLARK CO. LIMITED
TORONTO CANADA

The second Canadian printing of this title, circa 1941, conforms to the description given above under *The Land of Oz*. The dust jacket consists of plain heavy paper, blank on spine and flaps, to which has been pasted the cover paper pictorial label on front and back. (Bib. Oz. III; Schiller 167)

DOROTHY AND THE WIZARD IN OZ

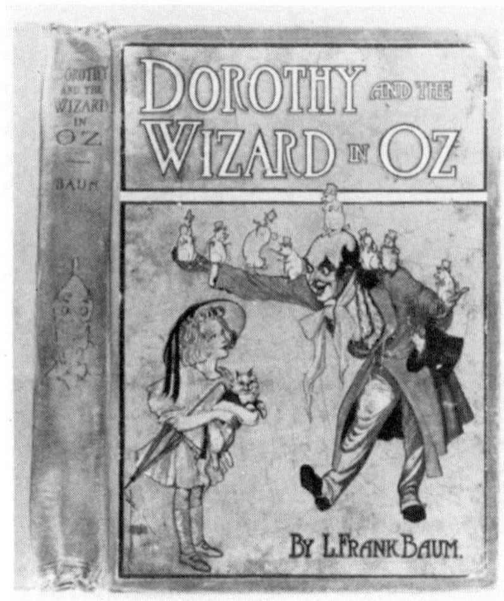

DOROTHY
AND THE WIZARD
IN OZ

BY

L. FRANK BAUM

AUTHOR OF THE WIZARD OF OZ, THE LAND OF OZ, OZMA OF OZ, ETC.

ILLUSTRATED BY

JOHN R. NEILL

Toronto
The Copp, Clark Co., Limited
Publishers

1908, identical to first American state except for either double or triple horizontal printer's rules at foot of spine rather than the publisher's imprint. Title page imprint 1. (Bib. Oz. IV; Schiller 179)

Spine imprint: Blank

Title page: Toronto/The Copp, Clark Co., Limited/Publishers

Later printing

circa 1941, conforms generally to the description of the first actual Canadian printings given above under *The Land of Oz*. The title-page imprint, however, differs, reading: "Toronto/The Copp Clark Co. Limited/Publishers," correcting the firm's name to its 1941 description. The colour-printed drawing on the dust jacket and the paste-down label omits the picture of Dorothy, as in U.S. issues of that period.

DOROTHY
AND THE WIZARD
IN OZ

BY

L. FRANK BAUM

AUTHOR OF THE WIZARD OF OZ, THE LAND OF OZ, OZMA OF OZ, ETC.

ILLUSTRATED BY

JOHN R. NEILL

Toronto
The Copp Clark Co. Limited
Publishers

THE ROAD TO OZ

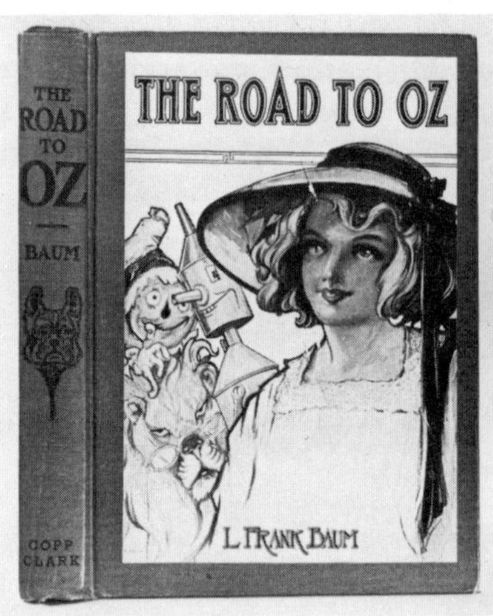

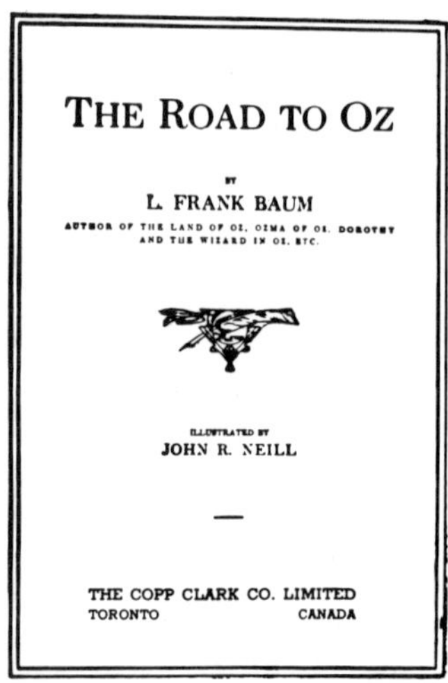
THE ROAD TO OZ

BY

L. FRANK BAUM

AUTHOR OF THE LAND OF OZ, OZMA OF OZ, DOROTHY AND THE WIZARD IN OZ, ETC.

ILLUSTRATED BY

JOHN R. NEILL

THE COPP CLARK CO. LIMITED
TORONTO CANADA

No evidence has been thus far discovered for the existence of a Copp Clark issue of *The Road to Oz* in 1909. The first recorded publication of *The Road to Oz* in Canada is the Canadian printing circa 1941. This printing conforms to the general pattern described under *The Land of Oz* above. Although this printing has blank endpapers, the fly leaves at front and back reproduce the drawing by John R. Neill originally intended for and appearing as the endpapers of *The Giant Horse of Oz* (1928) by Ruth Plumly Thompson. *The Road to Oz* is the only one of the Canadian-manufactured Oz books in this series to retain the spine vignette. (Bib. Oz. V; Schiller 193)

THE EMERALD CITY OF OZ

1910, identical to the first U.S. state in dark blue cloth, but with spine imprint I and title-page imprint 2. Copies have been reported in the Osborne Collection, Toronto Public Library, and the Beinecke Rare Book and Manuscript Library, Yale University. (Bib Oz. VI; Schiller 197)

Spine imprint: The Copp,/Clark Co.

Title page: PUBLISHERS/THE COPP, CLARK CO., LIMITED/TORONTO

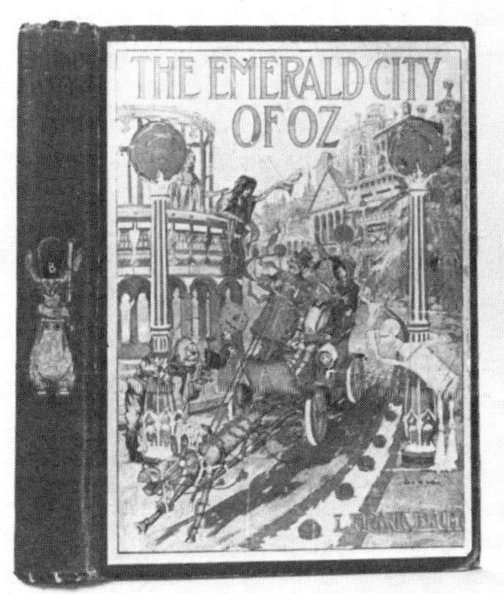

THE EMERALD CITY OF OZ

BY

L. FRANK BAUM

AUTHOR OF THE ROAD TO OZ, DOROTHY AND THE WIZARD IN OZ, THE LAND OF OZ, ETC.

ILLUSTRATED BY

JOHN R. NEILL

PUBLISHERS

THE COPP, CLARK CO., LIMITED

TORONTO

THE PATCHWORK GIRL OF OZ

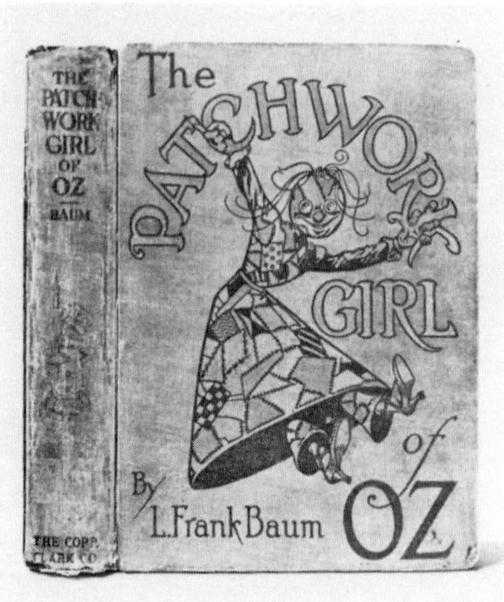

THE
PATCHWORK GIRL
OF OZ

BY
L. FRANK BAUM
AUTHOR OF THE ROAD TO OZ, DOROTHY AND THE WIZARD IN OZ, THE EMERALD CITY OF OZ, THE LAND OF OZ, OZMA OF OZ, ETC.

ILLUSTRATED BY
JOHN R. NEILL

THE COPP, CLARK CO., LIMITED
TORONTO

1913, identical to first American state in light green cloth, with "Chap. Three" repositioned to right of text. Spine imprint II and title-page imprint 3. McPherson Library, University of Victoria. (Bib. Oz. VII)

Spine imprint: THE COPP,/CLARK CO.

Title page: THE COPP, CLARK CO., LIMITED/ TORONTO

TIK TOK OF OZ

1914, identical to first U.S. state, including double horizontal rules at head and tail of spine; spine imprint III and title-page imprint 4. (Bib. Oz. VIII)

Spine imprint: THE/Copp, Clark Co./LIMITED

Title page: THE COPP, CLARK CO., LIMITED/ TORONTO

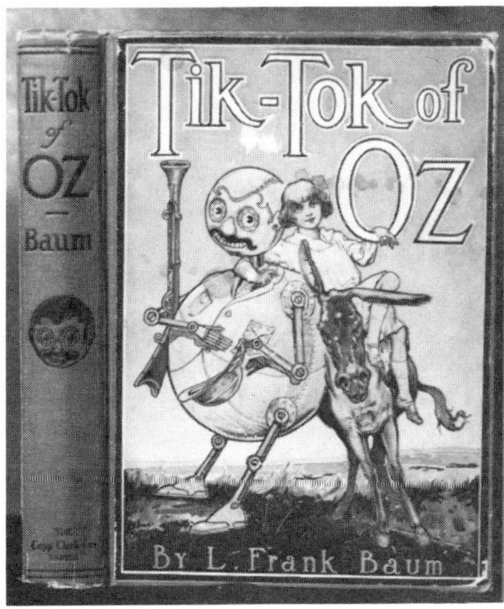

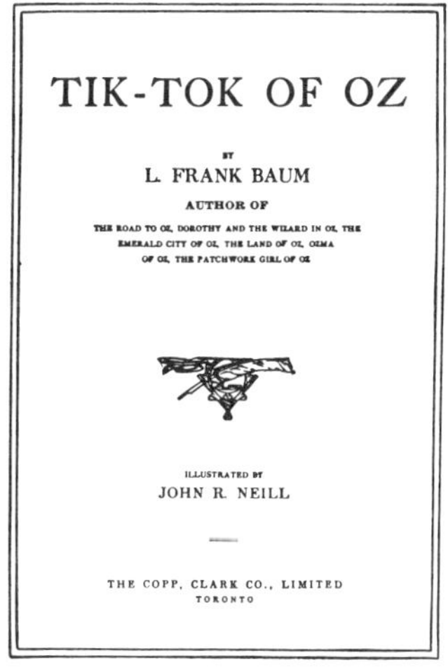

TIK-TOK OF OZ

BY

L. FRANK BAUM

AUTHOR OF

THE ROAD TO OZ, DOROTHY AND THE WIZARD IN OZ, THE EMERALD CITY OF OZ, THE LAND OF OZ, OZMA OF OZ, THE PATCHWORK GIRL OF OZ

ILLUSTRATED BY

JOHN R. NEILL

THE COPP, CLARK CO., LIMITED

TORONTO

THE SCARECROW OF OZ

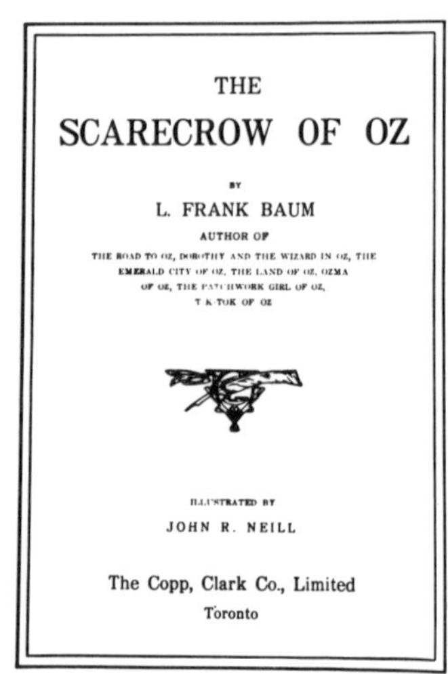

THE

SCARECROW OF OZ

BY

L. FRANK BAUM

AUTHOR OF

THE ROAD TO OZ, DOROTHY AND THE WIZARD IN OZ, THE EMERALD CITY OF OZ, THE LAND OF OZ, OZMA OF OZ, THE PATCHWORK GIRL OF OZ, TIK-TOK OF OZ

ILLUSTRATED BY

JOHN R. NEILL

The Copp, Clark Co., Limited

Toronto

1915, identical to first American state in bright green cloth; spine imprint IV and title-page imprint 6. The copy described here in the first recorded copy of the book. McPherson Library.

Spine imprint: THE COPP,/CLARK CO./LIMITED

Title page: The Copp, Clark Co., Limited/Toronto

RINKITINK IN OZ

1916, identical to first U.S. state, but with spine imprint IV and title-page imprint 6. "Made in U.S.A." has been added to the foot of copyright page: U.S. copies do not have this line. Because the U.S. copyright law required that books be manufactured in the United States in order to qualify for copyright protection, U.S. publishers customarily included a line indicating place of manufacture. *Rinkitink in Oz* is the only instance where the notice occurred only in the Canadian issue. In all other instances, if the U.S. copies bear the notice, it also appears in the Canadian copies. (Bib. Oz. X)

Spine imprint: THE COPP,/CLARK CO./LIMITED

Title page: The Copp, Clark Co., Limited/Toronto

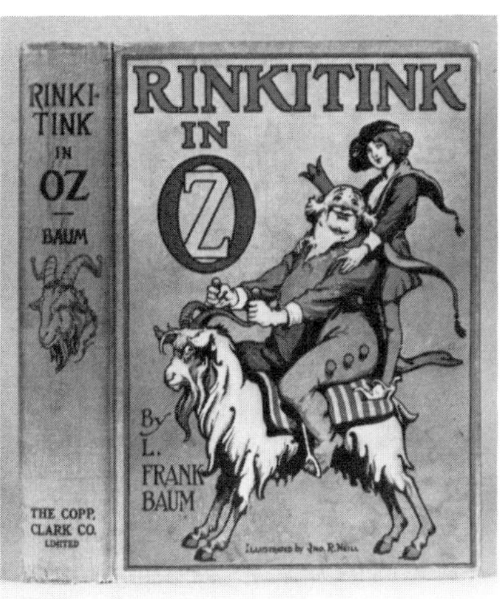

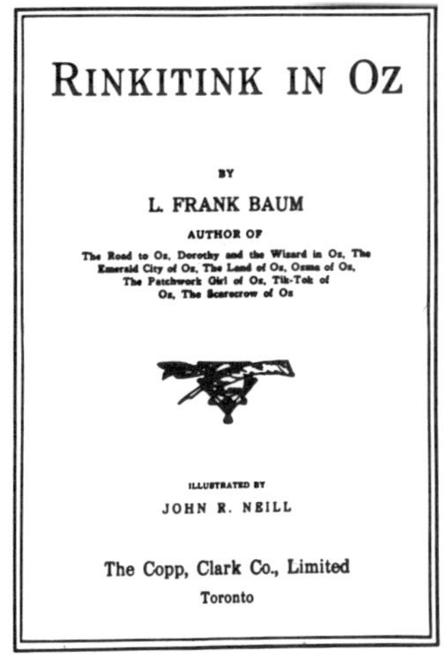

RINKITINK IN OZ

BY

L. FRANK BAUM

AUTHOR OF

The Road to Oz, Dorothy and the Wizard in Oz, The Emerald City of Oz, The Land of Oz, Ozma of Oz, The Patchwork Girl of Oz, Tik-Tok of Oz, The Scarecrow of Oz

ILLUSTRATED BY

JOHN R. NEILL

The Copp, Clark Co., Limited

Toronto

Copyright 1916
By L.Frank Baum

All Rights Reserved

Made in U. S. A.

THE LOST PRINCESS OF OZ

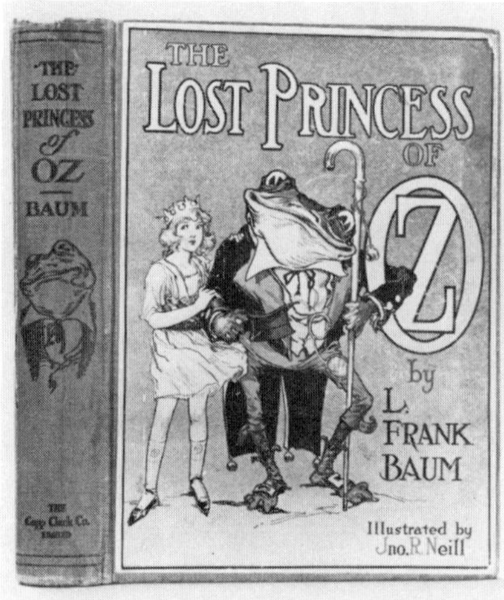

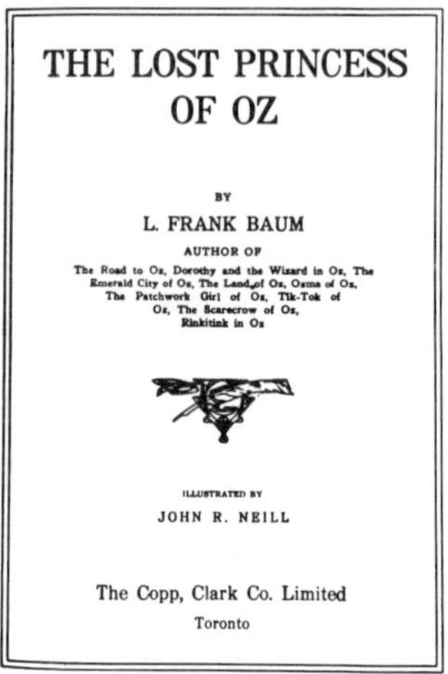

THE LOST PRINCESS
OF OZ

BY

L. FRANK BAUM

AUTHOR OF

The Road to Oz, Dorothy and the Wizard in Oz, The Emerald City of Oz, The Land of Oz, Ozma of Oz, The Patchwork Girl of Oz, Tik-Tok of Oz, The Scarecrow of Oz, Rinkitink in Oz

ILLUSTRATED BY

JOHN R. NEILL

The Copp, Clark Co. Limited

Toronto

1917, identical to first American state, including double horizontal rules at top and bottom of spine. Spine imprint III and title-page imprint 7. Foot of copyright page states "Made in U.S.A.", as in U.S. editions. (Bib. Oz. XI)

Spine imprint: THE/Copp Clark Co./LIMITED

Title page: The Copp, Clark Co. Limited/Toronto

THE TIN WOODMAN OF OZ

1918, identical to first U.S. state, but with spine imprint III and title-page imprint 5. "Made in U.S.A." in italics appears at foot of copyright page, as in U.S. editions. The copy described here is the first recorded copy of the book. McPherson Library.

Spine imprint: THE/Copp Clark Co./LIMITED

Title page: The Copp Clark Co., Limited/Toronto

THE TIN WOODMAN
OF OZ

A Faithful Story of the Astonishing Adventure Undertaken by the Tin Woodman, assisted by Woot the Wanderer, the Scarecrow of Oz, and Polychrome, the Rainbow's Daughter

BY

L. FRANK BAUM

"Royal Historian of Oz"

Author of
All the Oz Books

ILLUSTRATED BY
JOHN R. NEILL

The Copp Clark Co., Limited
Toronto

THE MAGIC OF OZ

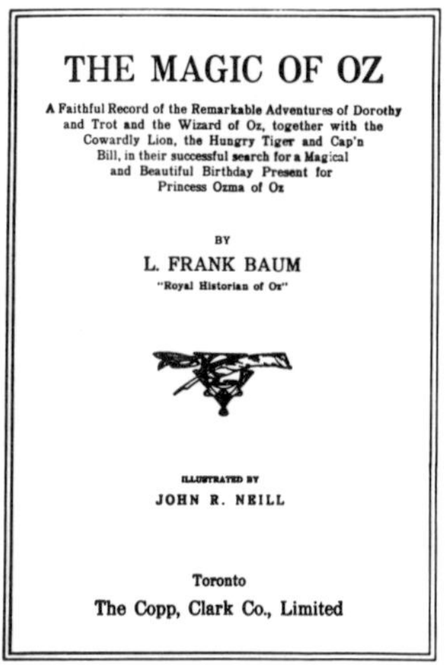

THE MAGIC OF OZ

A Faithful Record of the Remarkable Adventures of Dorothy and Trot and the Wizard of Oz, together with the Cowardly Lion, the Hungry Tiger and Cap'n Bill, in their successful search for a Magical and Beautiful Birthday Present for Princess Ozma of Oz

BY

L. FRANK BAUM

"Royal Historian of Oz"

ILLUSTRATED BY

JOHN R. NEILL

Toronto

The Copp, Clark Co., Limited

1919, identical to first American state in bright, emerald-green cloth, but with spine imprint III and title-page imprint 8. "MADE IN U.S.A." appears in hand-drawn letters at foot of copyright declaration, as in U.S. editions. (Bib. Oz. XIII)

Spine imprint: THE/Copp Clark Co./LIMITED

Title page: Toronto/The Copp, Clark Co., Limited

GLINDA OF OZ

1920, identical to first U.S. state in light brown cloth, but with spine imprint III and title-page imprint 9. Kerlan Collection, University of Minnesota. (Bib. Oz. XIV)

Spine imprint: THE/Copp Clark Co./LIMITED

Title page: Copp, Clark Co., Limited/Toronto

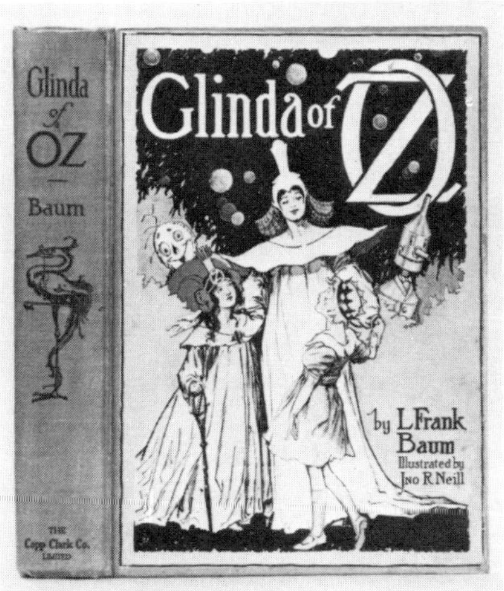

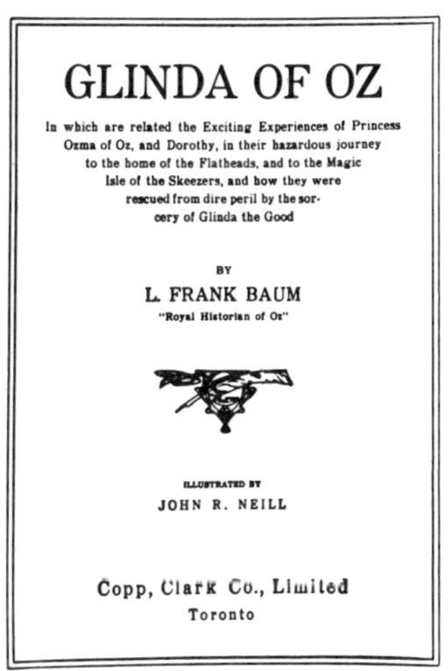

GLINDA OF OZ

In which are related the Exciting Experiences of Princess Ozma of Oz, and Dorothy, in their hazardous journey to the home of the Flatheads, and to the Magic Isle of the Skeezers, and how they were rescued from dire peril by the sorcery of Glinda the Good

BY

L. FRANK BAUM

"Royal Historian of Oz"

ILLUSTRATED BY

JOHN R. NEILL

Copp, Clark Co., Limited

Toronto

Later printing

circa 1960, the printer inadvertently created a new Copp Clark variant while filling a new printing order for Reilly & Lee. Evidently a set of printing plates for *Glinda of Oz* survived with the Copp Clark title-page imprint, for copies of the book were printed with the original Toronto imprint. The binding and dust jacket had the correct Reilly & Lee imprint. The introduction to this checklist gives the circumstances in greater detail. Light blue cloth, and at least one copy has a pictorial paste-down cover label hand-cut from the Dick Martin dust jacket. (Bib. Oz. pp. 17; Schiller 296) ____________________

THE ROYAL BOOK OF OZ

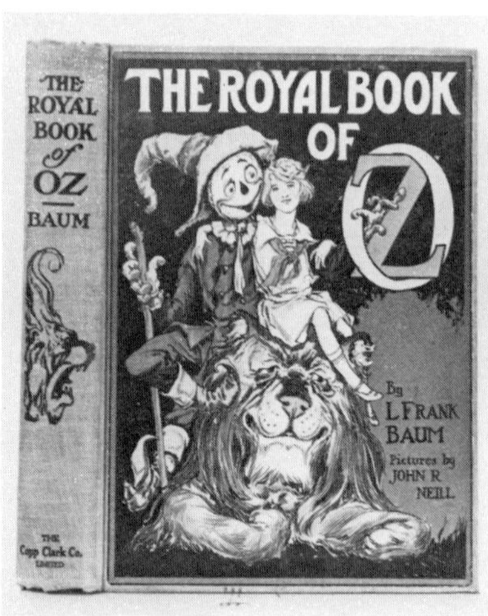

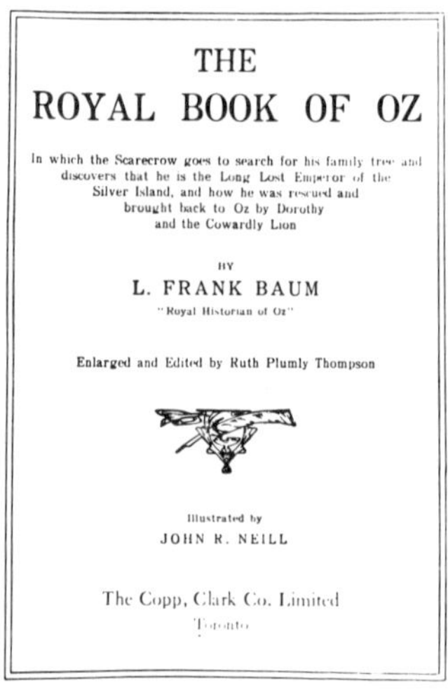
THE
ROYAL BOOK OF OZ

In which the Scarecrow goes to search for his family tree and discovers that he is the Long Lost Emperor of the Silver Island, and how he was rescued and brought back to Oz by Dorothy and the Cowardly Lion

BY

L. FRANK BAUM

"Royal Historian of Oz"

Enlarged and Edited by Ruth Plumly Thompson

Illustrated by

JOHN R. NEILL

The Copp, Clark Co. Limited

Toronto

1921, identical to first American state, but with spine imprint III and title-page imprint 7. "Made in U.S.A." appears in italics beneath the copyright notice, as in U.S. editions. The copy described here is the first recorded copy of the book.

Spine imprint: THE/Copp Clark Co./LIMITED

Title page: The Copp, Clark Co., Limited/Toronto

KABUMPO IN OZ

1922, identical to first U.S. state in blue-green cloth, but with spine imprint III and title-page imprint 10. Top of copyright page states "Printed in United States of America" in italics as in U.S. editions. *Bibliographia Oziana* reports that a metal printing

KABUMPO
IN OZ

BY
RUTH PLUMLY THOMPSON
Founded on and continuing the Famous Oz Stories
BY
L. FRANK BAUM
"Royal Historian of Oz"

Illustrated by
JOHN R. NEILL

The Copp, Clark Co., Limited
Toronto

plate for the Canadian spine was seen at the offices of Reilly & Lee used as a paperweight, but the copy described here is the first recorded copy of the book. Kerlan Collection. (Bib. Oz. XVI)

Spine imprint: THE/Copp Clark Co./LIMITED

Title page: The Copp, Clark Co., Limited/Toronto

THE COWARDLY LION OF OZ

1923, identical to first American state in deep emerald-green cloth, but with spine imprint III and title page imprint 11. "Printed in the United States of America" appears in italics at top of copyright page, as in U.S. editions. One colour-plate copy, apparently a binder's error, has the Canadian spine imprint, but a cancel Reilly & Lee title page. McPherson Library. (Bib. Oz. XVII)

Spine imprint: THE/Copp Clark Co./LIMITED
Title page: The Copp Clark Co. Limited./Toronto, Canada

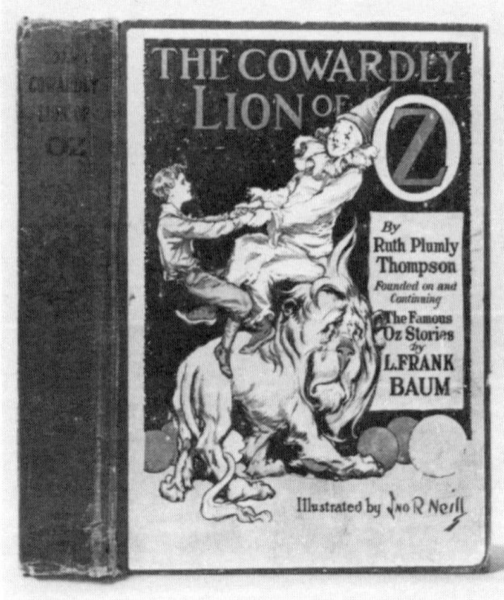

The Cowardly Lion of Oz

BY

RUTH PLUMLY THOMPSON

Founded on and continuing the Famous Oz Stories

BY

L. FRANK BAUM

"Royal Historian of Oz"

Illustrated by

JOHN R. NEILL

The Copp Clark Co. Limited.
Toronto, Canada

Later printing

circa 1960, a printer's error inadvertently resulted in the original Canadian title-page in these issues. Spine and dust jacket imprints are the correct Reilly & Lee impressions. Plain salmon pink cloth, with Dick Martin dust jacket. (Bib. Oz pp. 17)

GRAMPA IN OZ

Grampa In Oz

BY

RUTH PLUMLY THOMPSON

Founded on and continuing the Famous Oz Stories

BY

L. FRANK BAUM

"Royal Historian of Oz"

Illustrated by

JOHN R. NEILL

The Copp Clark Co. Limited

Toronto, Canada

1924, identical to first U.S. state, but with spine imprint V and title-page imprint 13. "Printed in United States of America" appears in italics at top of copyright page. The copy described here is the first recorded copy of the book. Kerlan Collection.

Spine imprint: Copp/Clark

Title page: The Copp Clark Co. Limited/Toronto, Canada

THE LOST KING OF OZ

The

Lost King of Oz

BY

RUTH PLUMLY THOMPSON

Founded on and continuing the Famous Oz Stories

BY

L. FRANK BAUM

"Royal Historian of Oz"

Illustrated by

JOHN R. NEILL

The Copp, Clark Co., Limited

Toronto, Canada

1925, identical to first American state, but with spine imprint VI and title-page imprint 14. Single copies have been seen with the top serif of the letter "k", page 193, line 4, both present and missing, apparently from the same press run. Top of copyright pages states "Printed in the United States of America", in italics and underlined, as in U.S. editions. (Schiller 296)

Spine Imprint: Copp,/Clark

Title page: The Copp, Clark Co., Limited/Toronto, Canada

THE HUNGRY TIGER OF OZ

1926, identical to first U.S. state, but with spine imprint VI and title-page imprint 15. Top of copyright page states "Printed in United States of America", in italics and underlined, as in U.S. editions. The copy described here is the first recorded copy of the book. Osborne Collection.

Spine Imprint: Copp,/Clark

Title page: The Copp, Clark Co., Limited/Toronto, Canada

The Hungry Tiger
of Oz

BY
RUTH PLUMLY THOMPSON
Founded on and continuing the Famous Oz Stories
BY
L. FRANK BAUM
"Royal Historian of Oz"

Illustrated by
JOHN R. NEILL

The Copp, Clark Co., Limited
Toronto, Canada

THE GNOME KING OF OZ

THE GNOME KING
of OZ

By
RUTH PLUMLY THOMPSON
Founded on and continuing the Famous Oz Stories
By
L. FRANK BAUM
"Royal Historian of Oz"

Illustrated by
JOHN R. NEILL

The Copp Clark Co., Limited
Toronto, Canada

THE GNOME KING
of OZ

By
RUTH PLUMLY THOMPSON
Founded on and continuing the Famous Oz Stories
By
L. FRANK BAUM
"Royal Historian of Oz"

Illustrated by
JOHN R. NEILL

The Copp Clark Co. Limited.
Toronto, Canada

1927, identical to first American state in bright, emerald-green cloth, but with spine imprint VI and title-page imprints curiously in either of two variants, 12 or 12a. The existence of two variant title-page imprints has not been explained, but suggests the possibility that damage to the original printing plate may have required resetting. No priority has been established, and in view of the normal distribution pattern, it is likely that both variants were released simultaneously. "Made in U.S.A." appears in italics at top of copyright page, as in U.S. editions. The copy described here is the first recorded copy of the book. Kerlan Collection.

Spine imprint: Copp,/Clark

Title page, variant 1: The Copp Clark Co. Limited/Toronto, Canada. variant 2: The Copp Clark Co., Limited./Toronto, Canada

---

THE GIANT HORSE OF OZ

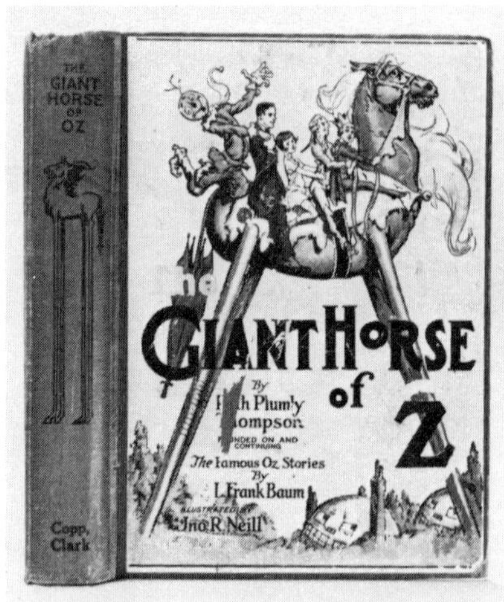

THE GIANT HORSE
of OZ

By
RUTH PLUMLY THOMPSON
Founded on and continuing the Famous Oz Stories
By
L. FRANK BAUM
"Royal Historian of Oz"

Illustrated by
JOHN R. NEILL

The Copp, Clark Co., Limited
Toronto, Canada

1928, identical to first U.S. state, but with spine imprint VI and title-page imprint 14. "Made in U.S.A." appears in italics at top of copyright page, as in U.S. editions. Kerlan Collection. (Bib. Oz. XXII)

Spine imprint: Copp,/Clark
Title page: The Copp, Clark Co., Limited/Toronto, Canada

JACK PUMPKINHEAD OF OZ

1929, identical to first American state, but with spine imprint VI and title-page imprint 16. Although a Copp Clark dust jacket for this title had been known for some time, the copy described here is the first recorded copy of the book. Kerlan Collection. (Bib. Oz. XXIII)

Spine imprint: Copp,/Clark

Title page: The Copp, Clark Co., Limited/Toronto, Canada

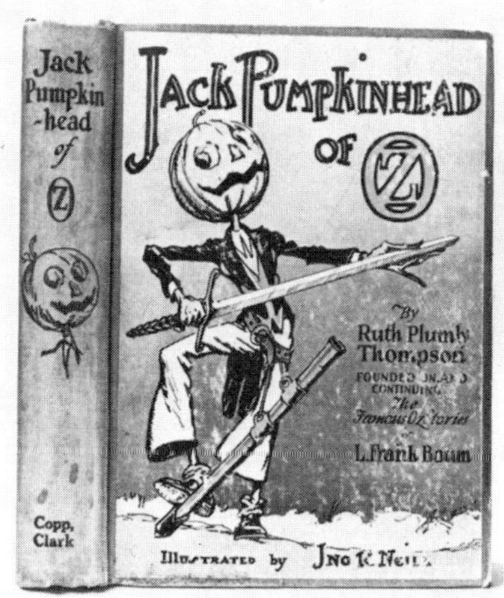

JACK PUMPKINHEAD
of OZ

By
RUTH PLUMLY THOMPSON
Founded on and continuing the Famous Oz Stories

By
L. FRANK BAUM
"Royal Historian of Oz"

Illustrated by
JOHN R. NEILL

The Copp, Clark Co., Limited
Toronto, Canada

THE YELLOW KNIGHT OF OZ

The
YELLOW KNIGHT
of OZ

By
RUTH PLUMLY THOMPSON
Founded on and continuing the Famous Oz Stories

By
L. FRANK BAUM
"Royal Historian of Oz"

Illustrated by
JOHN R. NEILL

The Copp, Clark Co., Limited
Toronto, Canada

1930, identical to first U.S. state in brick-red cloth, but with spine imprint VI and title-page imprint 14. The copy described here is the first recorded copy of the book. Kerlan Collection.

Spine imprint: Copp,/Clark

Title page: The Copp, Clark Co., Limited/Toronto, Canada

PIRATES IN OZ

1931, identical to first American state in medium-green textured cloth, but with spine imprint VI and title-page imprint 14. "Printed in the U.S.A." appears below copyright notice, as in U.S. editions. A variant colour-plate copy, evidently a binder's error, has been seen with the same title-page imprint, but a standard bold-face Reilly & Lee spine imprint. McPherson Library; Kerlan Collection. (Bib. Oz. XXV)

Spine imprint: Copp,/Clark

Title page: The Copp, Clark Co., Limited/Toronto, Canada

PIRATES in OZ

By

RUTH PLUMLY THOMPSON

Founded on and continuing the Famous Oz Stories

By

L. FRANK BAUM

"Royal Historian of Oz"

Illustrated by

JOHN R. NEILL

The Copp, Clark Co., Limited

Toronto, Canada

ADDENDA

EARLY CANADIAN ISSUES OF L. FRANK BAUM'S NON-OZ WORKS

QUEEN ZIXI OF IX

QUEEN ZIXI OF IX
Or, the Story of the Magic Cloak

BY
L. FRANK BAUM
AUTHOR OF "THE WIZARD OF OZ"

WITH ILLUSTRATIONS BY
FREDERICK RICHARDSON

TORONTO
THE COPP, CLARK COMPANY
LIMITED
1905

1905, identical to first U.S. state, as published by The Century Co., New York, including terra cotta and black illustrations on pages 169-236, inserted back endpapers, 16 tipped-in colour-plates and pictorial stamped binding designs on front, back and spine, but with spine imprint VII and title page imprint 18. Arkley Collection University of British Columbia (cf. "Bibliographia Baumiana, *The Baum Bugle,* Autumn 1969, and Spring 1970)

Spine imprint: THE/COPP, CLARK CO./LIMITED

Title page: TORONTO/THE COPP, CLARK COMPANY/ LIMITED/1905

THE SEA FAIRIES

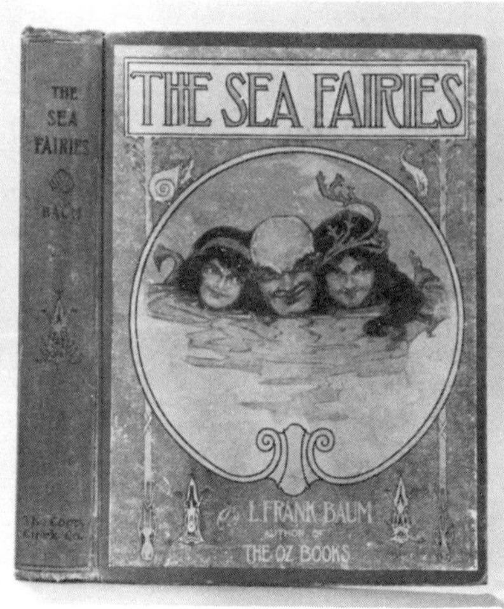

THE SEA FAIRIES

L. FRANK BAUM

JOHN R. NEILL

THE COPP, CLARK CO., LIMITED

1911, identical to first American state, including double horizontal rules enclosing a pink band, and seashell vignette on spine, but with spine imprint I and title-page imprint 17. McPherson Library. (cf. "Bibliographia Baumiana," *The Baum Bugle,* Spring 1970; Schiller 215)

Spine imprint: The Copp,/Clark Co.

Title page: TORONTO/THE COPP, CLARK CO., LIMITED/PUBLISHERS

SKY ISLAND

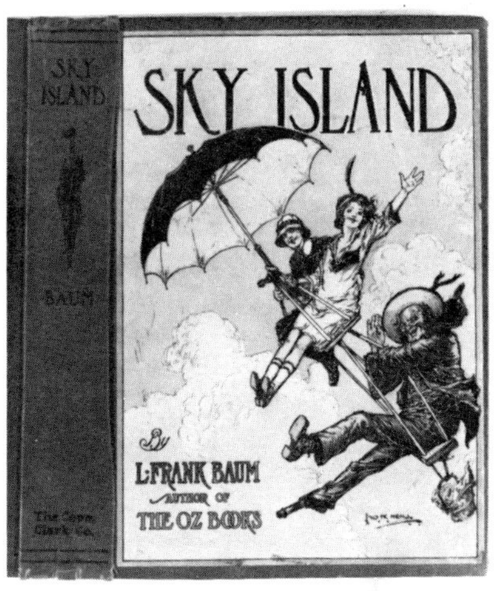

SKY ISLAND

Being the Further Exciting Adventures of Trot and Cap'n Bill after Their Visit to the Sea Fairies

By

L. FRANK BAUM

AUTHOR OF THE SEA FAIRIES, THE EMERALD CITY OF OZ, DOROTHY AND THE WIZARD IN OZ, OZMA OF OZ, THE ROAD TO OZ, THE LAND OF OZ, ETC.

ILLUSTRATED BY

JOHN R. NEILL

The Copp, Clark Co., Limited
Toronto

1912, identical to first U.S. state in brick-red cloth, including double horizontal rules at top and bottom of spine and red border surrounding paper pictorial label. Spine imprint I and title-page imprint 5. McPherson Library. (cf. "Bibliographia Baumiana," *The Baum Bugle,* Spring 1970)

Spine imprint: The Copp,/Clark Co.

Title page: The Copp, Clark Co., Limited/Toronto

PSEUDONYMA AND ANONYMOUS WORKS

PSEUDONYMA AND ANONYMOUS WORKS

THE FATE OF A CROWN

Schuyler Stanton, 1905. Reilly & Lee files are reported by Douglas G. Greene to have indicated that arrangements were made for a Canadian issue of *The Fate of a Crown*, but no copy of the book has yet been discovered. (cf. "Bibliographia Pseudonymiana," *The Baum Bugle,* Spring 1969)

THE LAST EGYPTIAN

Toronto: William Briggs, 1908. Identical to first American state, but with the Canadian publisher's imprint on the integral title page. Curiously, no effort was made to change the Philadelphia publisher's imprints elsewhere: the hybrid Canadian issue states "STERN" on the spine and "EDWARD STERN & CO. INC." at the foot of the pictorial paper cover label. (cf. "Bibliographical Anonymiana," *The Baum Bugle,* Spring 1970)

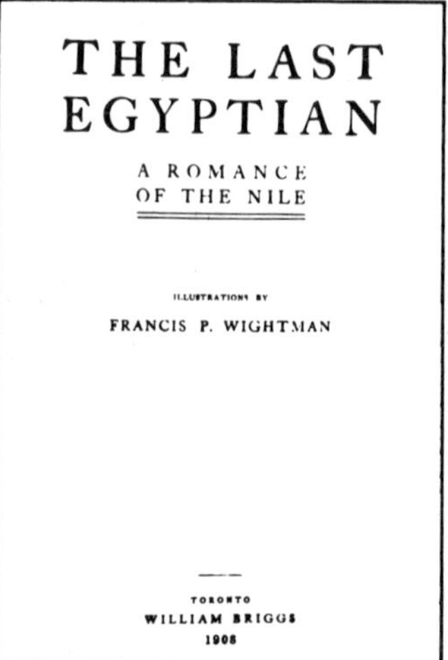
THE LAST
EGYPTIAN

A ROMANCE
OF THE NILE

ILLUSTRATIONS BY
FRANCIS P. WIGHTMAN

TORONTO
WILLIAM BRIGGS
1908

This is the only known early Canadian issue of a work by L. Frank Baum published by a company other than Copp Clark.
Spine imprint: STERN
Title page: TORONTO/WILLIAM BRIGGS/1908

AUNT JANE'S NIECES IN THE RED CROSS

Edith Van Dyne, 1915, identical to first U.S. state, but with Canadian spine and title-page imprints. The copy described still has its original dust jacket. Unfortunately, the area of the spine imprint has been torn off, but the back cover panel is an advertisement for books published by Reilly & Britton, so perhaps all the simultaneously produced Canadian first issues were distributed with Reilly & Britton / Reilly & Lee dust jackets. Strangely, this book is the only known Canadian title of the entire *Aunt Jane's Nieces* series.

Spine imprint: THE COPP,/CLARK CO./LIMITED
Title page: The Copp, Clark Co., Limited/Toronto

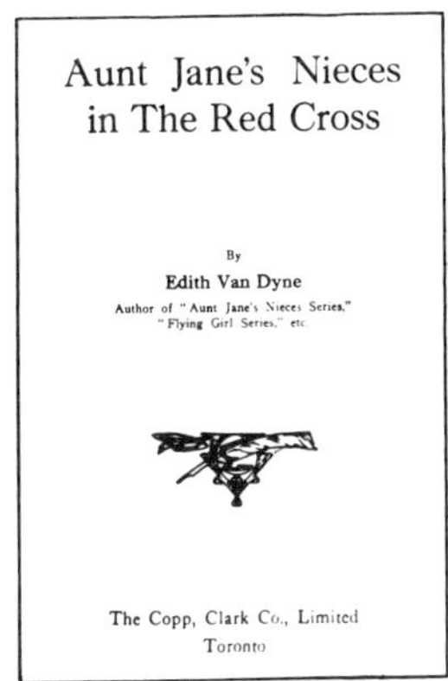
Aunt Jane's Nieces
in The Red Cross

By
Edith Van Dyne
Author of "Aunt Jane's Nieces Series,"
"Flying Girl Series," etc.

The Copp, Clark Co., Limited
Toronto

EPHEMERA

EPHEMERA

WONDERFUL GAME OF OZ, circa 1922, this board game is identical to the 1922 American Parker Brothers Oz Game, but with the Canadian imprint: MANUFACTURED IN CANADA BY / The COPP CLARK CO., Limited, Toronto.

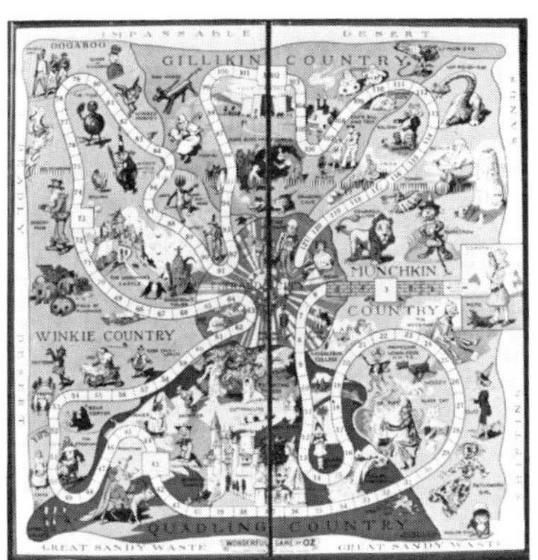

APPENDIX A. COPP CLARK SPINE IMPRINTS ON CANADIAN ISSUES OF FIRST EDITIONS

APPENDIX A.
COPP CLARK SPINE IMPRINTS ON CANADIAN ISSUES OF FIRST EDITIONS

I.
The Copp,/Clark Co.
The Emerald City of Oz, 1910
The Sea Fairies, 1911
Sky Island, 1912

II.
THE COPP,/CLARK CO.
The Patchwork Girl of Oz, 1913

III.
THE/Copp Clark Co./
LIMITED
Tik Tok of Oz, 1914
The Lost Princess of Oz, 1917
The Tin Woodman of Oz, 1918
The Magic of Oz, 1919
Glinda of Oz, 1920
The Royal Book of Oz, 1921
Kabumpo in Oz, 1922
The Cowardly Lion of Oz, 1923

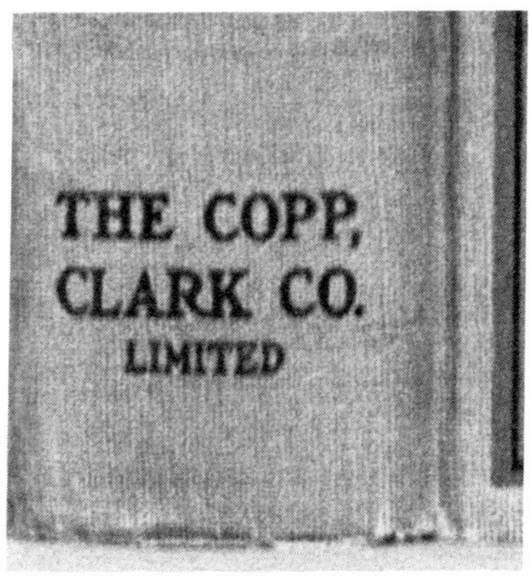

IV.
THE COPP,/CLARK CO./
LIMITED
The Scarecrow of Oz, 1915
Rinkitink in Oz, 1916

V.
Copp/Clark
Grampa in Oz, 1924

VI.
The Lost King of Oz, 1925
The Hungry Tiger of Oz, 1926
The Gnome King of Oz, 1927
The Giant Horse of Oz, 1928
Jack Pumpkinhead of Oz, 1929
The Yellow Knight of Oz, 1930
Pirates in Oz, 1931

VII.
THE/COPP, CLARK CO./
LIMITED
Queen Zixi of Ix, 1905

APPENDIX B.
COPP CLARK TITLE PAGE IMPRINTS OF CANADIAN ISSUES OF FIRST EDITIONS

APPENDIX B. COPP CLARK TITLE PAGE IMPRINTS OF CANADIAN ISSUES OF FIRST EDITIONS

1. *Toronto/The Copp, Clark Co., Limited/Publishers*

Toronto
The Copp, Clark Co., Limited
Publishers

Ozma of Oz, 1907
Dorothy and the Wizard in Oz, 1908

2. *PUBLISHERS/THE COPP, CLARK CO., LIMITED/ TORONTO*

PUBLISHERS
THE COPP, CLARK CO., LIMITED
TORONTO

The Emerald City of Oz, 1910

3. THE COPP, CLARK CO., LIMITED/TORONTO

THE COPP, CLARK CO., LIMITED
TORONTO

The Patchwork Girl of Oz, 1913

4. THE COPP, CLARK CO., LIMITED/TORONTO

THE COPP, CLARK CO., LIMITED
TORONTO

Tik Tok of Oz, 1914

5. The Copp, Clark Co., Limited/Toronto

The Copp, Clark Co., Limited
Toronto

The Tin Woodman of Oz, 1918
Sky Island, 1912
Aunt Jane's Nieces in the Red Cross, 1915

6. *The Copp, Clark Co., Limited/Toronto*

The Copp, Clark Co., Limited
Toronto

The Scarecrow of Oz, 1915
Rinkitink in Oz, 1916

7. *The Copp, Clark Co. Limited/Toronto*

The Copp, Clark Co. Limited
Toronto

The Lost Princess of Oz, 1917
The Royal Book of Oz, 1921

8. *Toronto/The Copp, Clark Co., Limited*

Toronto
The Copp, Clark Co., Limited

The Magic of Oz, 1919

9. Copp, Clark Co., Limited/Toronto

Copp, Clark Co., Limited
Toronto

Glinda of Oz, 1920

10. The Copp, Clark Co., Limited/Toronto

The Copp, Clark Co., Limited
Toronto

Kabumpo in Oz, 1922

11. The Copp Clark Co. Limited./Toronto, Canada

The Copp Clark Co. Limited.
Toronto, Canada

The Cowardly Lion of Oz, 1923

12. *The Copp Clark Co., Limited/Toronto, Canada*

The Copp Clark Co., Limited
Toronto, Canada

The Gnome King of Oz, 1927, variant 1

12a. *The Copp Clark Co., Limited./Toronto, Canada*

The Copp Clark Co. Limited.
Toronto, Canada

The Gnome King of Oz, 1927, variant 2

13. *The Copp Clark Co. Limited/Toronto, Canada*

The Copp Clark Co. Limited
Toronto, Canada

Grampa in Oz, 1924

14. The Copp, Clark Co., Limited/Toronto, Canada

The Copp, Clark Co., Limited
Toronto, Canada

The Lost King of Oz, 1925
The Giant Horse of Oz, 1928
The Yellow Knight of Oz, 1930
Pirates in Oz, 1931

15. The Copp, Clark Co., Limited/Toronto, Canada

The Copp, Clark Co., Limited
Toronto, Canada

The Hungry Tiger of Oz, 1926

16. The Copp, Clark Co., Limited/Toronto, Canada

The Copp, Clark Co., Limited
Toronto, Canada

Jack Pumpkinhead of Oz, 1929

17. TORONTO/THE COPP, CLARK CO., LIMITED/ PUBLISHERS

TORONTO
THE COPP, CLARK CO., LIMITED
PUBLISHERS

The Sea Fairies, 1911

18. TORONTO/THE COPP, CLARK COMPANY/LIMITED/1905

TORONTO
THE COPP, CLARK COMPANY
LIMITED
1905

Queen Zixi of Ix, 1905

REFERENCES

Bibliographia Oziana: A Concise Bibliographical Checklist of the Oz Books by L. Frank Baum and His Successors, by Peter E. Hanff and Douglas G. Greene, founded on and continuing the *Baum Bugle* checklists by Dick Martin, James E. Haff and David L. Greene, Kinderhook, Illinois, USA, The International Wizard of Oz Club, first edition, 1976, second edition, 1981. (Bib. Oz.)

The Baum Bugle: A Journal of Oz, published quarterly by The International Wizard of Oz Club, P.O. Box 95, Kinderhook, Illinois 62345 USA; membership is $10.00 (U.S.) annually. (TBB)

The Distinguished Collection of L. Frank Baum and Related Oziana including W.W. Denslow formed by Justin G. Schiller. Auction sale number 1118, Thursday, November 2, 1978 at 10:00 A.M. and 2:00 P.M., Swann Galleries, 104 East 25th Street, New York, New York 10010 USA. (Schiller)

ACKOWLEDGEMENTS

The author wishes to thank Peter E. Hanff, the late James E. Haff, Douglas G. Greene, David L. Greene, Justin G. Schiller and Fred M. Meyer for their encouragement, suggestions and contributions; Herman and Judy Bieber, Dick Martin, Doug and Mary-Anne Brown, Frank Lummis, C. Warren Hollister, John Van Camp, David Lee Hofer, Philip Sloan, Alan N. Grossman, John A. McMulkin, Frank A. and Carl R. Mulvey, Anne E. McNaughton and M. Wallace Friedman for their contributions; and the following libraries and research institutions for reference to their collections: Kerlan Collection, Children's Literature Research Collections, University of Minnesota; Osborne Collection, Toronto Public Library; The National Library of Canada; Beinecke Rare Book and Manuscript Library, Yale University; and the Arkley Collection, University of British Columbia. Special thanks must go to M. Nancy Cutt, McPherson Library, University of Victoria, who has brought together a fine collection of children's books with love and dedication. Laura Jane Musser is also owed a debt of gratitude for her help.

Peter Hanff and the late Jim Haff collaborated unstintingly, sharing their technical knowledge of bibliography and their eye for detail and accuracy. Barbara West, secretary to Mr. Pitman at Copp Clark Limited contributed the details of the history of Copp Clark. Many thanks also to Doug Brown for the very Oz-zy pictorial cover and to Glen Erikson for his patient photographic expertise. Bill Hoffer, my friend and colleague, foresaw the need for this contribution to Canadian publishing.

I am responsible, of course, for any errors or omissions and would warmly appreciate any additions or corrections to this checklist as well as notification of any locations of additional Copp Clark copies for reference.

—C.J. Hinke, Venkatesa Library,
Wickanninish Island, Box 524
Tofino, B.C. V0R 2Z0 Canada

THE AUTHOR

C.J. Hinke is a yoga teacher, private librarian, dilettante bookseller and collector of children's books. His two children, Sarah, aged 9, and Simon, aged 7, can both be trusted alone with first editions. He is presently collaborating on the first Latin translation of *The Wonderful Wizard of Oz,* to be called *The Classical Wizard.*

This first edition
of OZ IN CANADA
was set in 12 point
Bembo type on a
Compugraphic IV
phototypesetting machine
in July 1982,
and has been printed
in an edition of
1000 sewn paperbound
copies. An
additional 26
lettered copies have
been handbound in cloth
by Courtland Benson,
Twin Doves Bindery,
Victoria, British Columbia.

The End

OZ